A TRUE EASTER

THE SYNOD OF WHITBY, AD 664

BENEDICTA WARD SLG

SLG Press
Convent of the Incarnation
Fairacres • Parker Street
Oxford OX4 1TB England
www.slgpress.co.uk

FAIRACRES PUBLICATIONS 151

ISBN 978-0-7283-0345-4
ISSN 0307-1405

Cover illustration
Manuscript illumination with scenes of Easter in an initial A by the Bolognese illustrator Nerius, fragment from an Italian Antiphonary, *c.* 1320. Owned and donated to Wikimedia Commons by the Metropolitan Museum, New York.

CONTENTS

PART ONE

In AD 664 a meeting was held at Whitby to discuss the date upon which Easter should be celebrated. Why discuss this old debate now? Partly out of love of the northern kingdom where it happened and of the writer who tells about it; but more than that, because the debate about Easter at Whitby in 664 shows how easily a secular appeal to uniformity can be confused with a theological concern for unity. In any group, there is always more beneath the surface of topics discussed. Those concerned with public life in church, state, and university are rapidly made aware of hidden pitfalls and opportunities similar to those in seventh-century Northumbria. A study of these texts shows both how the past can be manipulated by modern debates, and also how, in terms of their own times, quite a different conclusion about them should be reached.

The seventh century was the golden age of Christianity in Northumbria, and it is often suggested that its pivotal moment was in 664 at the meeting held at the abbey at Whitby to decide on the date on which the Northumbrians would celebrate Easter. This meeting has been presented often enough as a clash between two kinds of Christianity, as an antagonism that was continual and deep. This has led to the view that there was an irreconcilable difference between Irish and Roman missionaries, finally culminating in a clash between charismatic simplicity and legal power about the date of Easter. But it was in no way an anti-Irish, pro-Roman tussle. That was the view of churchmen in the nineteenth century concerned with their own problems about English-Roman church differences, and not of seventh-century

Northumbria.[1] It is a misconception which is now creating the fantasy of a 'Celtic spirituality'.[2] This 'looking-glass approach' to history is an instance of how division can be created by a reading of history which explores the past in order to find present problems there, not seeing the past in its own light. Concern for the Easter date was a much wider and profounder question than nationalism, and it also involved non-church matters which brought a demand not for unity but for uniformity. It was not seen by the participants as a quarrel between different styles of Christianity, institutional Roman and free-spirited Celt; both were concerned with the same problem and went about solving it in the same way. What united them was far more profound than what divided them.

There were at least two issues discussed at Whitby, not just one. There was the situation of two differing dates for the celebration of Easter. This was not a frequent or an obvious clash, and it does not seem to have been a cause for conflict previously. According to both Bede and Eddius Stephanus, it was highlighted at that moment by external and domestic matters:

> Queen Eanflæd and her people … observed (Easter) as she had seen it done in Kent. … Hence it is said that in these days it sometimes happened that Easter was celebrated twice in the same year, so that the king had finished the fast and was keeping Easter Sunday, while the queen and her people were still in Lent and observing Palm Sunday.[3]

---

[1] Cf. Edmund Bishop, *Liturgica Historica* (Clarendon Press, 1917), chapter 19, 'About an Old Prayer Book', pp. 384–391.

[2] Bookshops now stock shelves full of books on 'Celtic spirituality', many of which have nothing either Celtic or spiritual about them.

[3] Bede, *Ecclesiastical History of the English People*, ed. and trans. B. Colgrave and R. A. B. Mynors (Clarendon Press, 1969) (hereinafter referred to as EH), Bk. 3: 24, p. 297.

The other problem was two styles of haircut, something immediately seen, and therefore a more noticeable difference than Easter. External signs matter in non-writing societies, and whether the shaving was of the whole head, the circle at the back only, or the front only, was something visible and obvious.[4] Bede and Ceolfrith in their letter to Nechtan noted the hair-cut problem and while saying that it was not really vital to theology, argued their point of view as a matter of uniformity only.[5] It certainly mattered enough in England for Theodore to wait six months for his shaved hair to grow so that he could be re-tonsured before he came to take up his post as seventh archbishop of Canterbury.[6] Differences about the date of the celebration of Easter were less frequently noticed, but were theologically more important: the whole year depended on the date of Easter, with its preparatory days of Lent and the next fifty days of Pentecost, both times for baptism and the preparation for baptism. It was not possible, therefore, to wait to see each year when the full moon would be the Pascal moon; it was an astronomical problem of forecasting years ahead.

The main source for information about the Easter controversy in Northumbria is Bede's *Ecclesiastical History of the English People*. In his history of the English nation as a race new-born into Christ, Bede placed at the centre a chapter which gives an account of the discussion at the council of Whitby in 664 of the differing dates at which Easter was celebrated by the Christians of the new Roman and the old Roman-Irish traditions.[7] In book five he also quoted at length a letter to Nechtan, king of the Picts,

---

[4] *Apologia de Barbis*, CCSM. This contains three medieval treatises about beards and haircuts.

[5] EH, Bk. 5: 21, pp. 546–9.

[6] EH, Bk. 4: 1, p. 331.

[7] EH, Bk. 3: 25, pp. 295–309.

which contains a detailed explanation of the problem.[8] In the *Ecclesiastical History of the English People*, Bede told the story of a newly converted barbarian people, their history seen under the lens of the gospel, as they became part of the church which was living in the sixth and last age of the world. His interest in them was theological, and his account of the debates at Whitby reflect this. He was also an excellent mathematician[9] and wrote elsewhere about the astronomical as well as the spiritual aspect of the matter. His sources for his account were almost certainly oral reminiscences of those who had been there, which was for him a major historical source, as he explained in his Preface.[10] One written source he may have known was Eddius Stephanus' *Life of Saint Wilfrid,*[11]a much briefer account, though substantially the same as that of Bede; after all, Bede knew and had spoken with Wilfrid, the main participant.[12] There were other people still alive who had been there as well as Wilfrid. No historian can claim to be entirely impartial, but it would unfair to think of Bede as a blind supporter of a Roman-style tradition. In himself Bede represented Anglo-Saxon, Roman-Irish and Gaulish-Roman traditions. He was by birth an Anglo-Saxon, and he lived from the age of seven in the monastery founded on the Roman pattern

---

[8] EH, Bk. 5: 21, pp. 533–553. The letter is attributed to Ceolfrith, but there can be no doubt about Bede's involvement with the text.

[9] Bede, *De Temporibus,* in *Bedae opera didascalica,* ed. C. W. Jones, 3 vols. CCSL (Brepols, 1975–1980) (hereinafter referred to as BOD). For extensive discussion, cf. *Bedae opera de temporibus,* ed. with introduction by C. W. Jones (Medieval Academy of America, 1943), and *Bede: The Reckoning of Time,* trans. with introduction and commentary by Faith Wallis (Liverpool University Press, 1999).

[10] EH, Preface, pp. 3–7.

[11] Eddius Stephanus, *Life of St Wilfrid,* ed. and trans. Bertram Colgrave (Cambridge University Press, 1927).

[12] EH, Bk. 4: 19, pp. 391–393.

by the Anglo-Saxon thane Benedict Biscop with the significant dedication to St Peter and St Paul, the apostles who were celebrated as martyrs in Rome. There is in Bede's life and works a sense of wonder and delight at all the riches of Christian culture brought to his race by the missionaries from Gaul and Rome, but also an equal respect for much that came to the island from Rome through Ireland. He was formed by and devoted to the Mediterranean Latin tradition of Christianity, but he saw it as being received from more than one source: from Rome through Gaul, certainly, but also from Rome through Ireland. Bede's account of the council was therefore not likely to reflect anything other than this sense of unity.

The meeting was held in the royal foundation of the Irish monk Aidan and Hilda at Whitby, on the borders between Deira and Bernicia; it became the burial place of Anglo-Saxon kings of Northumbria. The meeting was called by Bede *synodus*, that is a meeting for consultation, but it was not necessarily a 'church council'. It seems more profitable to regard it as a meeting of the king and his thanes and the local bishop to decide about many things, rather than to see it in terms of later church councils such as Hatfield. It was called by the king, he presided and the language of most people present was English; Cedd was employed as a translator from both Irish and Latin. As with early church councils, such as Nicaea, the difference between a church council and a secular meeting should not be pushed too far; but this was the seventh and not the fourth century, and bishops were perfectly capable of calling their own councils for church affairs. Here there was no archbishop present: Deusdedit of Canterbury was ill and died in July that year[13] and there was a thirty-year vacancy at York, which in any case was not then an archbishopric. The bishops present were Cedd and Agilbert, both bishops without portfolio;

---

13 EH, Bk. 4: 1, p. 329.

there was also Colman, who was Oswy's local bishop of Lindisfarne and a monk of Iona.

When we look at who said what and why, it was all more
mixed than at first appears. It was, after all, not a matter of the
arrogant men from Rome baring their teeth at the simple Irish.
At the council of Whitby, who supported which side? There was
no clear-cut division among the participants in terms of nationalism. An epitome of the mingling of traditions is seen in Hilda, the
hostess on this occasion. Hilda was an Anglo-Saxon princess
(614-680), younger daughter of Hereric, nephew of Edwin of
Northumbria and of Breguswith. She was born while her father
was a prisoner in Elmet of the British, who later killed him by
poison. Before her birth, her mother, feeling a sense of great loss,
dreamt that she found 'a most precious necklace under her garment ... such a blaze of light that it filled all Britain with its grace
and splendour'.[14] Hilda was brought up at the court of the Anglo-
Saxon Edwin. One sister, Hereswith, married the Anglo-Saxon
king of East Anglia, then became a nun at the convent of Chelles
in Gaul.[15] Hilda was baptized with Edwin and his court on April
12th 627, aged thirteen, in the new church dedicated to St Peter
in York by Paulinus.[16] She was almost certainly part of the group
of nobles who fled south with the queen when Edwin was killed
by Æthelred in 633.[17] Thus, by birth one of the Anglo-Saxons, her
first experience of Christianity was of that brought by the Roman
missionaries, a tradition emphasized by her later life in Gaul and
Kent. In 647, twenty years later, when she was thirty-three, Hilda
decided to be a nun and went to her nephew in East Anglia for a
year, planning to join her sister in the Gaulish convent at Chelles.
But she came to know and revere the Irish missionary from Iona,

---

[14] EH, Bk. 4: 23, p. 411.
[15] EH, Bk. 4: 23, p. 407.
[16] EH, Bk. Ibid.
[17] EH, Bk. 2: 20, p. 205.

Aidan, and he persuaded her to stay in England: first as part of a new group at Hartlepool, then, when the abbess Heiu left for a life of greater seclusion, Hilda became abbess of Whitby.[18] Hilda was hostess to the council of Whitby where, though by birth and baptism and life in exile one would have expected her to be a Romanist, because of the influence of Aidan and Colman she in fact inclined towards the Irish side. In her life there is a mixture of Anglo-Saxon, Roman and Irish elements which blended together imperceptibly.

No clear line can be drawn about others either. Cedd, the Anglo-Saxon founder of Lastingham, was made bishop on Iona for the East Saxons and consecrated by the Irish, but he acted as a careful and impartial interpreter at Whitby. King Oswy who called the council was from an Anglo-Saxon royal house, had been baptised by the Irish, spoke Irish and was a close friend of Colman, but accepted in the end without hesitation the new Roman calculation. Wilfrid himself, the architect of the Roman arguments and the first Englishman to appeal to Rome, had been educated in the Irish monastery of Lindisfarne. Agilbert, who ordained Wilfrid priest, though born in Gaul, had been educated in Ireland. Prince Aldfrith who was a friend of Wilfrid, gave him the abbey of Ripon only after offering it to Eata of Melrose, 'who followed the Irish ways'.[19] The illegitimate son of an Anglo-Saxon king and an Irish princess, Aldfrith had been educated in Ireland, but supported and indeed initiated the Roman arguments at Whitby. Colman was an Irish monk of Iona appointed as bishop of Lindisfarne, but a friend of the Anglo-Saxon Oswy. James the Deacon was an Italian, a companion of Paulinus who had stayed behind in Northumbria in 633 for a year under persecution and then continued to live there in a land dominated by Iona and

---

[18] EH, Bk. 3: 23, pp. 404–9.
[19] EH, Bk. 3: 25, p. 299.

'instructed many in singing after the manner of Rome and the Kentish people';[20] a quiet, elderly musician, he was nevertheless a participant at Whitby with experience of all sides.

So almost everyone at Whitby had close and friendly contact with both Roman and Irish missionaries; it was not a clash of opposites, but an argument between friends on a matter, the importance of which united them far more than the details divided. There was no sense that Romans were good and Irish were bad. In this matter of the Easter date, what needed sorting out were errors of calculation, whoever did it. Likewise with conduct: no-one was judged as Roman, English or Irish; such divisions were not appropriate. Roman missionaries, Anglo-Saxons and Irish were all in their conduct as Christians praised for some things and not admired for others. For instance, the Irish were praised for many apostolic virtues, but there were facets of the Irish character that were not seen as admirable, even when linked to evangelical zeal. They were fervent preachers, but their readiness to correct others was not always an advantage. Perhaps a certain challenge and fierceness was needed in the lands of the Irish, where there had been Christians since the days of Patrick, but the English were not yet Christian; they 'needed the milk of the word'. So, when a fierce hell-fire preacher was sent to Northumbria from Iona, he was sent home again and replaced by the wiser Aidan.[21] The Irish temper was not even very efficacious between themselves: when Ronan, an Irishman who had been in Gaul and accepted the new calculations for Easter, argued with his compatriot on the subject, Finan of Iona, 'who was a man of fierce temper', he enraged him instead of convincing him by the way in which he disputed with him.[22] The worldly

---

[20] EH, Bk. 2: 20, p. 207.
[21] EH, Bk. 3: 5, p. 229.
[22] EH, Bk. 3: 25, pp.275–7.

life of the Anglo-Saxon nuns at Coldingham was rebuked by the Irishman Adamnan, with whom Bede had argued in a friendly way about the form of tonsure appropriate to monks;[23] he saw fire descending on their monastery even though they had begun under the care of the royal Anglo-Saxon queen Æbba, a friend of Cuthbert.

There were other tensions at Whitby, however, which influenced the outcome, and these were connected with the son and daughter of Oswy. Eanflæda, the wife of Oswy, may or may not have been present at the council, but was certainly a powerful influence on the Easter debate. Bertha, a Merovingian princess from Gaul, was her grandmother, and her mother was Æthelburgh, wife of Edwin, sister of Eadbald of Kent. Their daughter, Eanflæda, had been born on Easter day (new calculation) and offered at once by her father for Christian baptism, since he had escaped a murder attempt that night. She thus became the first Christian in Northumbria; Edwin and the rest were baptised next year in York minster.[24] The baby Eanflæda had been baptized by the Roman missionary Paulinus, a companion of Augustine. When Penda and Cædwalla ravaged Northumbria (633) and Edwin was killed, Æthelburgh and Paulinus took the family, including Eanflæda and probably her cousin Hilda, and fled before the pagans to live in Kent and Gaul where they continued to observe the new date for Easter.[25] Some years later, Eanflæda returned to Northumbria as the wife of Oswy. Their daughter was princess Alfleda, who was given by her father as soon as she was weaned to her kins-woman Hilda to be brought up at Whitby, as a thank-offering after his victory at the decisive battle of Winwead, on 15th November 655.[26] While the whole

---

[23] EH, Bk. 5: 22, p. 551.

[24] EH, Bk. 2: 14, p. 187.

[25] EH, Bk. 2: 20, p. 205.

[26] EH, Bk. 3: 24, p. 291.

experience of her mother had been rooted in the traditions of Gaul and Rome, by 664 Alfleda had lived for nine years in an Irish environment. There may have been no conflict about this, but when the question was raised, it is not at all likely that the queen would be content to continue to celebrate a different Easter from her daughter, especially since Easter, the day of her birth, was so significantly linked to the new Easter date. Later Eanflæda joined Alfleda as a nun at Whitby, where her daughter succeeded Hilda as abbess. Quite apart from the domestic difficulties of two Easter days and two periods of Lent, there was not the slightest chance that the problem would be resolved by Eanflæda changing her way of celebrating Easter.

The other family problem was posed by Alfleda's half-brother, Aldfrith. He had fought at his father's side at the Winwead as a good soldier, clever, able and ambitious, but he was a man without secure prospects. He had been given some authority in Deira while Oswy was expanding the northern borders, but Aldfrith had his own way to make. It seems probable that he raised the question of the two dates of Easter in order to discredit his father in public and show him as provincial and wrong about Easter, therefore undermining his Christian alliances in Kent and Gaul. He brought in the young Wilfrid to propose the arguments for the new Easter dating, having him ordained priest by Agilbert just before the council. Disappointed in his schemes at Whitby, Aldfrith then married Cynburgh, sister of Peada of Mercia, and raised a rebellion in the same year; when that failed, he disappeared from history.[27]

It was not a matter of taking sides in a theological dispute which had caused the Northumbrian kings to follow the Irish

---

[27] For another discussion of these issues see Henry Mayr-Harting in *The Coming of Christianity to Anglo-Saxon England* (Batsford, 1972), Chapter 7, 'The Synod of Whitby', pp. 103–113.

dating of Easter. After the year of chaos following the death of Edwin, there was bitter warfare between the pagan invaders and the new Christian claimant to the throne, Oswald, who, like his brother and successor Oswy, had been in exile and received Christian baptism from Irish monks on Iona. Oswald became king in Northumbria, and naturally at once introduced missionaries from Iona, who followed the conservative Irish customs. In one year, and with disciples of Paulinus still alive and active, the new calculation for the date of Easter was surely still assumed to be correct by many in Northumbria, but a difference came with the advent of the Irish-trained Oswald and Oswy and their new Irish missionaries, friends of the kings, who kept Easter as they had done on Iona, on a different day from the Roman missionaries, and indeed from the rest of the church. The second stage in the conversion of Northumbria, therefore, accidentally differed from the first in this one matter. Paulinus, Edwin, Æthelburgh and their daughter Eanflæda, later the wife of Oswy, naturally calculated according to the modern revised dating; Aidan and Oswald and Oswy equally naturally according to the unrevised dating, which had also originally come from Rome. It was an unconscious difference, but confusing for the Northumbrians. The politics of Oswy are easy to understand. The problems with a divided Easter in his household were as nothing compared to the risk of losing the alliances which his marriage represented. That the decision reached at Whitby was fruitful was immediately shown when later in the same year Egbert of Kent, the queen's uncle, and Oswy jointly sent Wigheard to Rome to be ordained as the next archbishop of Canterbury. Pope Vitalian then wrote congratulating Oswy on his conformity about Easter, and mentioning warmly Eanflæda's part in the matter.[28] Oswy was well aware

---

[28] EH, Bk. 3: 29, pp. 319–323.

of latent problems concerning his wife and her relations in Kent and Gaul. He was no less alert to the possibility that his son could demonstrate through the debate that his father was concerned only with that area of Christianity in Northumbria dominated by Iona, while he himself would assert his wider alliances through Wilfrid. Well aware of issues quite other than the calculation of Easter Day, Oswy began the council with a reference to the need for unity throughout the whole church. At the end, he turned the tables on his son by claiming the exact position Aldfrith had hoped to gain, speaking, as Eddius says, *subridens*, with a secret smile.

> When Wilfrid had ended his speech, King Oswy said, 'Is it true, Colman, that the Lord said these words to Peter?' Colman answered, 'It is true, O king. ... Do you all agree, without any dispute, that these words were primarily addressed to Peter and that the Lord gave him the keys of the kingdom of heaven?' They both answered 'Yes'. Thereupon the king concluded, 'Then I tell you, that since he is the doorkeeper I will not contradict him ... lest when I come to the gates of the kingdom of heaven there may be no-one to open them.'[29]

In matters of political alliance and credibility as high king on a large scale, Oswy was no-one's fool. But with such undercurrents to manage, it was no wonder he had been rather thoughtful when the council opened.

The Synod of Whitby decided the actual issue of the date of Easter on spiritual authority rather than argument, but it was the details of the calendar, which was by no means foremost at the synod, which Bede drew out and explained. As he knew from Eusebius,[30] the date of Easter had occupied the mind of the early church. The council of Nicaea had decreed that Easter should

---

[29] EH, Bk. 3: 25, p. 307.
[30] Eusebius, *De Vita Constantini*, 3: 18, (85. 26–37).

always be observed on a Sunday.[31] How to determine *which* Sunday had, however, remained a problem, to be solved by astronomers as much as by theologians and biblical scholars. In England there had been one initial clash between the Roman missionaries and the British, that is to say the Welsh Christians. Augustine wrote to ask advice from Pope Gregory about his relationship with them and received the reply:

> We commit to you, my brother, all the bishops of Britain that the unlearned may be instructed, the weak strengthened by your counsel, and the perverse corrected by your authority.[32]

Augustine therefore invited the Welsh bishops to a conference and urged them: 'that they should preserve catholic peace with him and undertake the joint labour of evangelizing the heathen for the Lord's sake'.[33] After a long dispute, in which the calculation of the date of Easter was mentioned, 'they were unwilling, in spite of the prayers, exhortations and rebukes of Augustine, and his companions, to give their assent, a stance which they maintained after a further long discussion, saying also that "they would not preach the way of life to the English nation"'. The contacts between the Christians in Wales and the mission to the Anglo-Saxons seemed to have ceased thereafter. A demand for uniformity from a stance of power had resulted in deep and lasting division. At first the Welsh were simply old-fashioned in calculating Easter and therefore at variance with the more up-to-date tables from Rome, but as a result of the confrontation with Augustine, it became for them a sign of their individuality.

But with the Irish it was different, and any conflict over jurisdiction and the authority of Augustine did not flare up in his

---

[31] For the view of the Council of Nicaea, cf. N. Tanner, *Decrees of the Ecumenical Councils*, vol. 1 (Sheed and Ward, 1990), p. 19.

[32] EH, Bk. 1: 27, pp. 87–89.

[33] EH, Bk. 2: 2, p. 139.

lifetime. In 664, over one hundred years after the coming of both Augustine and the Roman mission and Aidan and the Irish, a point of disagreement about the date at which Easter should be celebrated each year was seen to divide them; but it had in no way prevented joint evangelization earlier. The golden age of Northumbria in the seventh and eighth centuries, one of the most amazing flowerings of Christian culture known, was based on an Anglo-Saxon Northumbria filled with Irish and with Roman missionaries, and in other kingdoms the contacts between them were also basic. It is a false dichotomy to see English and Irish in opposition in these early centuries. The true picture is of a pagan culture, that of the Anglo-Saxons, in touch with Christian culture in two ways, one from Rome through Gaul, one from Rome through Ireland. The southern Irish had already accepted the new calculations before Whitby. Why some of the Irish and also some of the English differed from the new missionaries about this crucial date was not a matter of alternative symbolism or theology or biblical study, but of the authority for the two calendric calculations. It was not, as Wilfrid suggested at Whitby, because the Irish were Quartodecimans, that is, those who kept the feast of Easter on any day of the week, provided it was the fourteenth of Nisan. The Irish calculated Easter in a perfectly orthodox manner; the problem was that they were using lunar tables which had reached them from Rome but had been replaced elsewhere. Other minor differences also caused the dates sometimes to coincide, sometimes to be a week apart, sometimes four weeks apart. To Anglo-Saxon Christians such differences had been by and large tolerable until the issue was raised, and after 664 they and most of the Irish agreed to observe together the new dating for Easter; by 731 even the conservative Iona had followed suit.

Why some of the Irish and also some of the English differed from the new Roman missionaries about this crucial date was a matter of their loyalty to the tradition of Columba, but behind it lay the more fundamental problem of calendric calculation. The question was about the date of the Paschal full moon after the Vernal equinox, a combination of solar and lunar calendars which even electronic calculators cannot solve. This question was answered by the adoption of cycles of years. The first person to draw up such a cycle was Victorius of Aquitaine, whose work was adopted in Rome about 457. It comprised 532 years, starting with the supposed date of the crucifixion, and ran from AD 28 to AD 559. This cycle was improved upon by Dionysius Exiguus, who drew up a cycle which ran from 1 BC to AD 532 and from AD 532 to AD 1063. In 525 he had produced a table for calculating Easter based on the lunar cycle of 532 years; that is, twenty eight periods of nineteen years each, reckoned from the year of the birth of Christ.[34] This was finally adopted by the Church, but it was not and still is not entirely satisfactory; Bede wrote extensively about the problems involved, but in his account of the debate at Whitby, calendric matters were not central, nor would they have been any more comprehensible to the court than they are to ourselves.

The results of the Synod's decision were to determine the alliances and orientation of the church in Britain, but there was no scapegoating of those who refused to change. Colman indeed resigned his bishopric and returned to his monastery, but in a sense he had no option; a monk and bishop holding his authority from Iona, he naturally returned there with some English and some Irish monks. He took with him some of the bones of Aidan, but also left some of them in Lindisfarne. Significantly, Oswy showed his respect for Colman by asking him to name his successor as bishop (Tuda) and as abbot (Eata). The chapter following Bede's

---

[34] Admirably discussed by Faith Wallis, *Bede: The Reckoning of Time* (Liverpool University Press, 1999).

account of Whitby was devoted to the highest praise of Colman as an apostolic servant of God.[35] Respect for Columba, Aidan and Colman had surrounded the debate. The community on Iona continued to keep the 'true Easter of Columba'.[36] Built as they were on the immense authority of the holiness of their saints, they were not moved by royal decrees from Whitby, nor changed by Ronan and Finan's debates; they were equally un-moved by Adamnan's arguments. But in 729 a very respected English Irish-trained monk, Egbert, voluntarily abandoned his way of life and went and lived humbly on Iona. Respect for him led to discussion, and he was able to show them why it was in line with their own traditions that they should change. He died on the first Easter day calculated in the new way to be cele-brated on Iona; a change that had nothing to do with politics and everything to do with prayer, holiness and humility.[37]

Issues are always more complex than doctrine only. There were domestic and political problems at the northern court There were problems for mission in Northumbria, where the two dates for the Easter feast made differences about baptism. There were practical problems about the calendric calculations to be resolved. Bede, looking back at the debate, stressed what concerned him; that is, the unity of all round the resurrection and the importance of astronomical calculations being correct. Time leading into eternity, non-time, nevertheless has its own dimensions, and these mattered. Numbers are as important as words.[38] But every-one involved, of different backgrounds and traditions, agreed in their devotion to Easter as the central feast of the Resurrection.

---

[35] EH, Bk. 3: 26, pp. 309–11.

[36] *Adamnan's Life of St Columba*, ed. and trans. A. O. Anderson and M. Anderson (Nelson, 1962), Bk. 1: 3, p. 219.

[37] EH, Bk. 5: 22, p.555.

[38] Cf. Alexander Murray in *Reason and Society in the Middle Ages* (Oxford University Press, 1978), pp. 146–7.

With this basic unity in mind, they were able to discuss how they were to look towards Jesus as the risen Lord, and so they emerged from the debate without hating each other. Where those who differed from the majority of Christians did so in ignorance, while their conduct and prayer remained sound, Bede himself did not deal out condemnation. He wrote, for instance, of Aidan, his ideal among monks:

> All these things I greatly admire and love in this bishop. ... I neither praise nor approve of him insofar as he did not observe Easter at the proper time. ... I do approve of this, that in his celebration of Easter he had no other thought in his heart, he reverenced and preached no other doctrine than we do, namely the redemption of the human race by the passion, resurrection and ascension into heaven of the one mediator between God and men even the man Jesus Christ.[39]

In conclusion, the meeting at Whitby shows that no divisive situation is ever resolved by discussion of divisive topics alone, but by the depth of love and prayer and respect for what already unites. It is perhaps not without interest to see how the outcome of this debate, with all its peculiarities, in fact imbued the Anglo-Saxons afterwards with a greater devotion than ever for the central and uniting fact of the resurrection. As new converts, the Anglo-Saxons had not found the idea of a festival in spring entirely new, and they saw a connection between the date of the Pasch and their custom of celebrating a spring goddess; in his book on time, Bede refers to the Anglo-Saxon name for the feast of the Resurrection:

> Easter-month, which is now called the paschal month, was formerly so called from a goddess of theirs (the English) called Eostre and since her festival was celebrated then it had that

---

[39] EH, Bk. 3: 17, p. 267.

name. By that name they now call the time of Pascha, customary observance giving its name to a new solemnity.[40]

The name has remained pagan, as indeed did the Anglo-Saxon word 'Lent' (spring), which is still used rather than the Latin *jejunium* (the fast); the days of the week likewise did not become the series of ferias after the first day of Sunday, but remain obstinately dedicated to Woden, Thor and Freya. The names remained, but in each case the content was radically different. Not the words but the content mattered; as Bede said, 'I thank you, good Jesu, for turning us from such vanities, and allowing us to offer the sacrifice of praise'. Not that the date of the death and resurrection of Jesus was a myth, or in any way arbitrary; it was an historical fact in time, and because of it, all time was changed into a new configuration. The date depended primarily on the scriptures, but tradition had linked the date into the ebb and flow of the universe, of all creation, and it is not surprising to find that one of Bede's most intense passages on the calculation of Easter occurs in his commentary on the account of the creation of the world in Genesis. In his first book on the calculation of time, he linked the date of Easter with the created world in detail: the Pasch, he says, is central to creation as well as to redemption:

> when the equinox is passed, that the shadow of death may be vanquished by the true light, … in the first month of the year, which is called the month of New Fruits, so that the joy of a new life may be celebrated … at the turn of the moon, to show how the glory of the mind is turned from earthly things to heavenly ones … on the Lord's Day, when the light shows the triumph of Christ and our own resurrection.[41]

---

[40] *Bede: The Reckoning of Time*, ed. and trans. Faith Wallis (Liverpool University Press, 1999), cap.15, pp. 53–4.

[41] Bede, *De Temporibus* cap.xv, 'On the Sacrament of the Pascal Season', BOD, 123a. p. 599.

In the Letter to Nechtan he added:

> We are commanded to keep the full moon of the paschal
> month after the vernal equinox, the object being that the sun
> should first make the day longer than the night and then the
> moon can show to the world her full orb of light because 'the
> Sun of righteousness with healing in his wings' (Mal. 4:2) that
> is, the Lord Jesus, overcame all the darkness of death by the
> triumph of his resurrection.[42]

To secure unity which flowered into uniformity was not the
same as imposing uniformity; and whatever the superficial mo-
tives and schemes of those present may have been, the true unity
forged at Whitby was a turning point indeed for Anglo-Saxon
Christianity. An incipient difference, which could have been
used by secular ambitions, was resolved by patience and respect
all round, so that unity about what mattered most could eventu-
ally produce a true uniformity. The proof of this is to be found in
the continued English love of Easter, which produced a flowing
of energy from the resurrection into art, drama and poetry:

> For at the dawning there came a throng of angels,
> the rapture of those hosts surrounded the Saviour's tomb,
> The earthly vault was opened,
> the Prince's corpse received the breath of life;
> the ground shook and hell's inhabitants rejoiced.
> The young man awoke dauntless from the earth;
> the mighty Majesty arose, victorious and wise.[43]

---

42 Bede, EHEP Bk. 5: 21, p. 545.
43 *Anglo-Saxon Poetry*, 'The Descent into Hell', trans. S. A. J. Bradley
(Dent, 1982), p. 392.

PART TWO

THE PROBLEMS OF THE EASTER CONTROVERSY
IN THE WRITINGS OF THE VENERABLE BEDE
A Simplified Guide

A. *Bede's Discussion of the Date of Easter:*

Ecclesiastical History of the English People

Book 3, cap. xxv: Arguments used at the Council of Whitby.

Book 5, cap. xxi: Letter of Ceolfrith to Nechtan, King of the Picts.

Commentary on Genesis, 17–18: commenting on the creation of the sun and moon, pp. 15–20.

Commentary on Luke, VI, xxii, 7–8 (p. 375).
Commentary on Mark, IV, xiv, 12 (p. 609).
De Temporum Ratione, caps. v, viii, xix, lxiv.
De Temporibus: full discussion of paschal calculation.
De Natura Rerum, ix-xiv (pp. 206–299).
Letter to Wicthed, xi (p. 324).

B. *Methods of Calculating Easter in Eighth-Century Northumbria*

POINTS OF AGREEMENT

i.   Easter must be celebrated on a Sunday.
ii. It must fall in the first lunar month of the year.
iii. It must be after the Vernal Equinox, i.e. the day in the solar year when the number of hours of daylight equal the hours of darkness after which the hours of daylight increase.
iv. It must be after the first full moon after the Vernal Equinox.

POINTS OF DIFFERENCE

i.   XIV Nisan

Romans:

> This was the day the Jews celebrated Passover, whatever the day of the week. It was not permissible to celebrate a Sunday as Easter if the Passover also occurred on that day; it was deferred to the next Sunday.

Celts:

> It was permissible to celebrate Easter on a Sunday on which Passover was also celebrated.

> Every seventh year this could result in the difference of a week between the two Easter celebrations.

ii. The Vernal Equinox

> Romans kept it on March 21st.

> Celts kept it on March 25th.

iii The first full moon after the Vernal Equinox

1st Difference

Romans:

> The Paschal moon was that which became full after March 21st; if the moon was full before March 21st that was not deemed to be the Paschal moon and the next lunar month was then regarded as the first month of the year and that moon as the Paschal moon.

Celts:

> The Paschal moon was the one full after March 25th.

2nd Difference

Romans:

> began the liturgical day on the evening before, so the Sunday after the full moon after the Vernal Equinox (March 21st) was not regarded as Easter Day if the full moon occurred after

midnight; in this case Easter would be celebrated on the next Sunday, a week later.

Celts:

began each day in the morning, so if the full moon after the Vernal equinox rose at any time on the night of Saturday to Sunday, the Celts would keep that Sunday as Easter.

Therefore:

Romans:

Possible days in the lunar month for Easter were xv–xxi Nisan. Possible days in the year for Easter Day were March 22–April 25.

Celts:

Possible days of the lunar month for Easter were xiv–xx Nisan. Possible days of the year for Easter Day were March 24–April 22.

C. *Examples*

1. Romans and Celts might celebrate Easter **on the same day** when, for example, the new moon was March 12th (Thursday) and the full moon March 26th (Wednesday). The Vernal Equinox was either March 21st or March 25th. Therefore, Easter Day would be the first Sunday after the full moon after the Equinox, which for both would be March 30th.

2. They might celebrate Easter **a week apart** when, for example, the new moon was March 19th (Saturday) and the full moon April 2nd, which fell on Sunday after midnight. The Vernal Equinox was either March 21st or March 25th. Celtic Easter would be April 2nd, the same night; Roman Easter would be April 9th, a week later.

3. They might celebrate Easter **four weeks apart** when, for example, the new moon was March 8th (Sunday), and the full moon March 22nd (Friday). Vernal Equinox was either March 21st or March 25th. As the full moon came *after* the Roman Vernal Equinox of March 21st, the Roman Easter would be

the following Sunday, March 24th. But the full moon would be *before* the Celtic Vernal Equinox of March 25th, so this would not be for them the first full moon after the Vernal Equinox. They would, therefore, not count that as the month Nisan but wait for the next new moon to be full and would celebrate four weeks later. Celtic Easter would be April 21st.

Note: if Passover was celebrated on a Sunday of the first full moon after March 25th, the Celts would postpone Easter for a week.

(The present differences between Orthodox Easter and Western Easter depend upon the choice of the Julian Calendar or the Gregorian Calendar, where there is fourteen days difference in calculating the Vernal Equinox.)

SLG PRESS PUBLICATIONS

CONTEMPLATIVE POETRY SERIES

VESTRY GUIDES

slgpress.co.uk